MW00638217

ISBN: 978-1-66783-604-1

If You Were Here

For my miracles in
Heaven and on Earth

By Shonal Narayan
Illustrations by Ricky Audi

Mommy and Daddy
say you're an angel.
But if you were here,
I think we'd be best friends.

If you were here,
I'd teach you about bugs.
We'd **explore** and catch butterflies,
beetles and slugs.

If you were here,
we'd ride our bikes all day.
And build the coziest pillow forts
to nestle and play.

We'd close our eyes,
create adventures and **make-believe**.

We'd be unicorns and elves,
and other enchanted beings.

Like, if you were a dinosaur,
WOW! Imagine that.
We'd stomp 'round the house
and roar at the cat.

If you lived in a **magical** pond
as a colorful koi fish,
I'd dip my fingers in the water
and make a **kind wish**.

If you were a **Shooting Star**,
I'd love to watch you fly.
I'd stand on a hill to catch you,
as you **Shimmered** across the sky.

What if you were a race car?
That would be so Cool!
I'd be at every one of your races
So proud to Cheer for you.

And even if
you were a
grouchy goblin...

a **Stinky** onion...

or a prickly cactus,
I'd always be by your side.

Our extraordinary life together
would be one amazing ride.

But since we never met,
I didn't have the chance to say...

we are family and I love you,
no matter what you'd be today.